Super Bowl LIX Recap

The Eagles' Dominance, Kendrick Lamar's Halftime Show, and Football History

Lewis Snyder

CONTENTS

INTRODUCTION.. **5**

    The Road to Super Bowl LIX.............................5

    A Historic Matchup...7

Chapter 1: The Journey to Super Bowl LIX...... 11

    Season Highlights for the Eagles and Chiefs..11

    Key Players and Team Dynamics................... 15

    Pre-game Build-Up and Predictions...............21

Chapter 2: Game Day Highlights...................... 25

    Stadium Atmosphere and Opening Ceremonies
    25

    First Half Key Moments...................................27

    Tactical Insights and Team Performance........ 30

Chapter 3: The Second Half and Victory.......... 41

    Turning Points of the Game........................... 41

    Game-Changing Plays.....................................45

    Final Score and Eagles' Triumph................... 50

**Chapter 4: Standout Performances and Records
56**

    Jalen Hurts' MVP Moment............................. 56

    Saquon Barkley's Contributions......................59

    Key Defensive Players and Historical
    Achievements...63

**Chapter 5: The Halftime Show and Cultural
Impact.. 69**

    Kendrick Lamar's Performance Highlights......69

    Special Guest Appearances............................ 74

    Social and Cultural Significance..................... 78

Chapter 6: Post-Game Celebrations and Legacy.

81

Player and Coach Reactions............................81
Media and Fan Responses.............................. 86
The Legacy of Super Bowl LIX........................ 89
CONCLUSION...**95**

INTRODUCTION

The Road to Super Bowl LIX

Super Bowl LIX, held on February 9, 2025, at the Caesars Superdome in New Orleans, showcased a thrilling matchup between the Philadelphia Eagles and the Kansas City Chiefs. This game was not only a testament to the teams' exceptional performances throughout the season but also a rematch of their previous Super Bowl encounter, adding an extra layer of anticipation and excitement.

Philadelphia Eagles' Journey
The Eagles entered the postseason as the second seed in the NFC. Their playoff journey began with a victory over the Green Bay Packers, followed by a win against the Los Angeles Rams. In the NFC Championship, they faced the Washington Commanders, securing their spot in the Super Bowl with a decisive 55-23 win. This marked their second Super Bowl appearance in three years, underscoring the team's consistent excellence.

Kansas City Chiefs' Path
The Chiefs, holding the top seed in the AFC, commenced their playoff run with a win against the

Houston Texans. They then faced the Buffalo Bills in the AFC Championship, emerging victorious with a close 32-29 scoreline. This victory propelled them into their third consecutive Super Bowl, a feat that highlighted their dominance in recent years.

Season Highlights and Key Players
Throughout the season, both teams demonstrated remarkable skill and resilience. Eagles' quarterback Jalen Hurts delivered outstanding performances, culminating in his recognition as the Super Bowl MVP. On the other side, Chiefs' quarterback Patrick Mahomes continued to showcase his exceptional talent, leading his team to yet another Super Bowl appearance.

Anticipation and Stakes
The lead-up to Super Bowl LIX was filled with anticipation, not only because it was a rematch but also due to the Chiefs' pursuit of a historic third consecutive Super Bowl win. Fans and analysts eagerly awaited the clash, speculating whether the Chiefs would cement their dynasty or if the Eagles would avenge their previous loss and claim the championship.

In summary, the road to Super Bowl LIX was paved with intense competition, strategic prowess, and standout performances from both the Philadelphia

Eagles and the Kansas City Chiefs. Their journeys through the season and playoffs set the stage for a highly anticipated and memorable championship game.

A Historic Matchup

Super Bowl LIX will forever be remembered as a clash between two NFL powerhouses, the Philadelphia Eagles and the Kansas City Chiefs, marking one of the most eagerly anticipated rematches in Super Bowl history. Both teams were not only vying for the prestigious Vince Lombardi Trophy but also for the chance to cement their respective legacies in the annals of professional football. With compelling narratives, dynamic rosters, and high stakes on both sides, this historic matchup captured the attention of football fans and analysts worldwide.

The Philadelphia Eagles: A Season of Redemption

The Eagles entered Super Bowl LIX on a mission to reclaim their championship glory after narrowly missing the title in previous years. Under the leadership of their determined quarterback, Jalen Hurts, the Eagles had a season defined by resilience, strategic gameplay, and standout performances. Their offense was one of the most dynamic in the league, with Hurts' dual-threat ability as both a passer and a rusher giving opposing defenses nightmares.

Philadelphia's defense was equally formidable, known for its aggressive pass rush and disciplined secondary. Throughout the season, the Eagles demonstrated their ability to win high-stakes games, earning the respect of the league and solidifying their reputation as championship contenders. Their path to the Super Bowl was marked by impressive victories over top NFC teams, making their presence in Super Bowl LIX well-deserved.

The Kansas City Chiefs: Pursuing a Dynasty

The Kansas City Chiefs, led by the electrifying Patrick Mahomes, were on the brink of making NFL history. With two consecutive Super Bowl victories already under their belt, they entered Super Bowl LIX with hopes of achieving a rare three-peat—a feat that had not been accomplished in the modern NFL era. The Chiefs' high-octane offense, spearheaded by Mahomes' unparalleled arm talent and playmaking ability, made them a perennial threat on the field.

The Chiefs also boasted a resilient defense that had stepped up in critical moments throughout the season. With a well-balanced team and a coaching staff led by the highly respected Andy Reid, the Chiefs were determined to continue their reign as champions and cement their dynasty in professional football. Their journey to the Super Bowl included hard-fought battles against formidable AFC opponents, showcasing their grit and determination.

A Rematch for the Ages

What made this matchup even more historic was its status as a rematch of a previous Super Bowl encounter. The Chiefs and Eagles had faced off in a thrilling championship game just two years prior, with the Chiefs emerging victorious. The loss had lingered in the minds of the Eagles, fueling their motivation to seek redemption and rewrite the narrative.

This rematch carried emotional weight for players and fans alike. The rivalry between the two teams had grown stronger, and the anticipation for their showdown at Super Bowl LIX reached a fever pitch. Analysts and commentators speculated endlessly about which team would come out on top, dissecting every aspect of their gameplay, strategies, and key matchups.

The Stakes and Legacy Implications

Beyond the immediate goal of winning the Super Bowl, the stakes were incredibly high for both teams. For the Eagles, a victory would signify their return to dominance and validate their hard work and perseverance over the past seasons. It would also bolster Jalen Hurts' reputation as one of the league's elite quarterbacks.

For the Chiefs, the pursuit of a third consecutive championship was about more than just a trophy—it was about solidifying their dynasty and etching their names in the history books alongside the greatest teams of all time. A win would further elevate Patrick Mahomes' legacy, placing him among the NFL's all-time great quarterbacks.

A Game for the Ages
The historic matchup between the Philadelphia Eagles and the Kansas City Chiefs at Super Bowl LIX promised to be a spectacle filled with high drama, intense competition, and unforgettable moments. As the two teams prepared to face off, fans and football enthusiasts braced themselves for a game that would be talked about for years to come. Super Bowl LIX was not just a championship game—it was a defining moment in NFL history, where legacies were made, and legends were born.

Chapter 1: The Journey to Super Bowl LIX

Season Highlights for the Eagles and Chiefs

The road to Super Bowl LIX was filled with drama, determination, and remarkable performances for both the Philadelphia Eagles and the Kansas City Chiefs. Each team faced challenges but proved their mettle, earning their place on the grandest stage of professional football.

Philadelphia Eagles: A Season of Redemption
The Eagles entered the 2024 NFL season with a chip on their shoulders. After a disappointing 2023 campaign that saw them miss the playoffs, the team made several key changes. One of the most significant moves was acquiring star running back Saquon Barkley from the New York Giants. Barkley's presence added depth to their offense and provided a spark that the team desperately needed.

Under the leadership of head coach Nick Sirianni and quarterback Jalen Hurts, the Eagles quickly established themselves as a dominant force in the league. Hurts showcased remarkable growth, demonstrating poise in the pocket and the ability to make plays with his legs. His connection with wide receivers DeVonta Smith and A.J. Brown proved to be one of the most formidable duos in the league.

Defensively, the Eagles were a force to be reckoned with. Their defensive line, led by Fletcher Cox and Haason Reddick, consistently pressured opposing quarterbacks, while the secondary, bolstered by the emergence of Cooper DeJean, made game-changing plays. DeJean, in particular, became a fan favorite for his timely interceptions and aggressive playstyle.

The Eagles finished the regular season with a 14-3 record, securing the top seed in the NFC. They carried that momentum into the playoffs, defeating the San Francisco 49ers and the Dallas Cowboys to punch their ticket to the Super Bowl.

Kansas City Chiefs: A Bid for a Historic Three-Peat

The Kansas City Chiefs entered the 2024 season as the defending Super Bowl champions, having won back-to-back titles in 2022 and 2023. With head coach Andy Reid and star quarterback Patrick Mahomes at the helm, the Chiefs were once again favored to make a deep playoff run.

Mahomes continued to dazzle with his incredible arm strength, pinpoint accuracy, and ability to extend plays. His connection with tight end Travis Kelce remained one of the most productive partnerships in the league. Despite losing key wide receivers in the offseason, Mahomes elevated the performance of his supporting cast, turning young talents into reliable playmakers.

Defensively, the Chiefs made significant improvements under coordinator Steve Spagnuolo. Chris Jones anchored the defensive line, while the secondary, led by L'Jarius Sneed, consistently disrupted opposing offenses.

The Chiefs finished the regular season with a 13-4 record, earning the top seed in the AFC. Their playoff journey was marked by thrilling victories, including a nail-biting win against the Cincinnati Bengals in the AFC Championship game. As they prepared for Super Bowl LIX, the Chiefs were determined to achieve a rare three-peat and solidify their dynasty status.

A Clash of Titans

The stage was set for an epic showdown between two of the league's most formidable teams. The Eagles, hungry for redemption, and the Chiefs, seeking to cement their legacy, promised a game filled with high stakes and intense competition. With star players like Jalen Hurts and Patrick Mahomes at the forefront, and seasoned coaches Nick Sirianni and Andy Reid orchestrating their strategies, fans around the world eagerly anticipated one of the most memorable Super Bowl matchups in recent history.

This season's journey for both teams was a testament to their resilience, talent, and determination to reach the pinnacle of professional football. The stage was now set for a historic battle that would be remembered for years to come.

Key Players and Team Dynamics

Super Bowl LIX featured two powerhouse teams with a rich mix of veteran stars, rising talents, and strategic masterminds on the coaching staff. The success of both the Philadelphia Eagles and the Kansas City Chiefs was driven by the exceptional contributions of key players and the well-coordinated dynamics within their rosters.

Philadelphia Eagles: A Well-Balanced Team with Firepower

The Eagles entered the 2024 season determined to redeem themselves after a disappointing previous year. Their success hinged on a dynamic offensive lineup, a fearsome defense, and strong leadership from their coaching staff.

Jalen Hurts (Quarterback)

Hurts emerged as a true leader for the Eagles. His ability to throw deep, execute quick passes, and make plays with his legs made him one of the most versatile quarterbacks in the league. Hurts demonstrated resilience throughout the season, often leading the team to victory in high-pressure situations. His strong connection with the Eagles' top receivers made the offense a formidable force.

Saquon Barkley (Running Back)

The Eagles' acquisition of Saquon Barkley proved to be a game-changer. Known for his explosive speed, elusive running style, and ability to catch passes out of the backfield, Barkley added a new dimension to the Eagles' offense. He consistently broke through defenses, racking up yards and touchdowns. His contribution not only strengthened the running game but also took pressure off Hurts.

DeVonta Smith and A.J. Brown (Wide Receivers)

Smith and Brown formed one of the most dynamic receiving duos in the league. Smith's precise route-running and reliable hands complemented

Brown's physicality and ability to make contested catches. Together, they provided Hurts with reliable targets and stretched opposing defenses.

Defensive Powerhouses

Haason Reddick (Edge Rusher)

Reddick was a nightmare for opposing quarterbacks. His ability to disrupt the backfield with sacks and tackles for loss made him a key figure in the Eagles' defensive success. His aggressive playstyle and leadership energized the entire defensive unit.

Fletcher Cox (Defensive Tackle)

A veteran leader on the defensive line, Cox used his experience and strength to anchor the Eagles' defense. His ability to stop the run and pressure quarterbacks made him a cornerstone of the team's front seven.

Cooper DeJean (Defensive Back)

DeJean became a standout player in the secondary. His instinct for reading plays and making critical interceptions earned him recognition as one of the top young defenders in the league. His contributions helped solidify the Eagles' defensive backfield.

Kansas City Chiefs: A Well-Oiled Machine Led by Mahomes

The Chiefs, on the other hand, continued to build on their dynasty aspirations under the leadership of head coach Andy Reid and quarterback Patrick Mahomes. Their success was a result of a balanced approach on both sides of the ball.

Offensive Stars

Patrick Mahomes (Quarterback)

Mahomes remained the face of the franchise and one of the most electrifying players in the NFL. His ability to make impossible throws and extend plays under pressure made him a constant threat. Despite losing key wide receivers in the offseason, Mahomes elevated the performance of his supporting cast, turning young players into reliable targets.

Travis Kelce (Tight End)

Kelce continued to be Mahomes' most trusted target. His ability to find openings in defenses, make tough catches, and gain yards after the catch made him a nightmare for opposing teams. His chemistry with Mahomes was evident throughout the season.

Isiah Pacheco (Running Back)

Pacheco emerged as a reliable and explosive running back. His aggressive running style and ability to break tackles provided balance to the Chiefs' offense, allowing Mahomes to operate more effectively.

Defensive Stalwarts

Chris Jones (Defensive Tackle)

Jones was the anchor of the Chiefs' defense. His ability to generate pressure from the interior and stop the run made him one of the most dominant defensive linemen in the league.

L'Jarius Sneed (Cornerback)

Sneed played a crucial role in the Chiefs' secondary. His versatility allowed him to cover top receivers and make key plays in crucial moments. His leadership and experience were invaluable to the defensive unit.

Coaching Strategies and Team Dynamics

Nick Sirianni (Philadelphia Eagles Head Coach)

Sirianni's leadership was a key factor in the Eagles' success. He created a game plan that maximized the strengths of his star players and fostered a winning culture. His ability to adapt to different game situations and motivate his players made him one of the top coaches in the league.

Andy Reid (Kansas City Chiefs Head Coach)
Reid's reputation as an offensive genius was once again on display. His ability to design creative plays and keep opposing defenses guessing was instrumental in the Chiefs' success. Reid's calm demeanor and experience in high-stakes games provided stability to the team.

Both teams had unique dynamics that contributed to their success. The Eagles relied on a balanced approach with strong offensive and defensive units, while the Chiefs leaned on Mahomes' brilliance and Reid's tactical expertise. The clash between these two well-constructed teams set the stage for a thrilling Super Bowl LIX showdown.

Pre-game Build-Up and Predictions

As the countdown to Super Bowl LIX intensified, the atmosphere around the NFL was electric. Football analysts, sports enthusiasts, and die-hard fans were engaged in heated debates, speculating on the strategies and outcomes of what promised to be a legendary showdown between the Philadelphia Eagles and the Kansas City Chiefs. The media frenzy was at an all-time high, with every aspect of the game dissected and scrutinized.

Media Coverage and Fan Excitement

The media played a crucial role in building anticipation for the big game. Sports networks aired round-the-clock coverage, featuring interviews with players, coaches, and analysts. ESPN, Fox Sports, and NFL Network provided in-depth analysis, predicting key matchups and discussing each team's strengths and weaknesses.

Social media platforms were abuzz with fan predictions and commentary. Hashtags like #SuperBowlLIX, #EaglesNation, and #ChiefsKingdom trended globally. Fans created memes, shared highlight reels, and engaged in debates about which team would emerge victorious.

The excitement was palpable not only in Philadelphia and Kansas City but across the entire United States and beyond. Super Bowl parties were being planned, with fans eager to witness one of the most anticipated matchups in recent history.

Team Preparations

Both teams arrived at the Super Bowl with a laser focus on preparation. The Philadelphia Eagles and the Kansas City Chiefs held intense practice sessions, reviewing game footage and refining their strategies.

Philadelphia Eagles

The Eagles' head coach, Nick Sirianni, emphasized a disciplined approach. He stressed the importance of executing plays flawlessly and maintaining composure under pressure. Quarterback Jalen Hurts was seen leading drills with precision, ensuring that his offensive line was in sync.

The Eagles' defense, led by Haason Reddick and Fletcher Cox, spent countless hours studying the Chiefs' offensive plays. Their goal was clear: disrupt Patrick Mahomes and limit his ability to make explosive plays.

Sirianni's strategy focused on a balanced attack, utilizing Saquon Barkley's dynamic running game to complement Hurts' passing ability. The Eagles' coaching staff also placed significant emphasis on special teams, knowing that a single play could change the course of the game.

Kansas City Chiefs

The Chiefs' preparation was characterized by innovation and adaptability. Head coach Andy Reid, known for his offensive genius, worked closely with Mahomes to design creative plays that could catch the Eagles' defense off guard.

Travis Kelce, the team's star tight end, was a focal point in their game plan. The Chiefs' offensive line was tasked with protecting Mahomes and creating opportunities for Isiah Pacheco in the running game.

Defensively, the Chiefs concentrated on containing Jalen Hurts and disrupting his connection with wide receivers DeVonta Smith and A.J. Brown. Chris Jones, a dominant force on the defensive line, led the charge in preparing to pressure Hurts and shut down the Eagles' rushing attack.

Key Storylines and Predictions
As game day approached, several key storylines captured the attention of fans and analysts:

The Quarterback Duel:
The showdown between Jalen Hurts and Patrick Mahomes was one of the most anticipated matchups in recent Super Bowl history. Hurts was coming off an MVP-caliber season, while Mahomes was already regarded as one of the greatest quarterbacks of his generation. Analysts debated whether Hurts' dual-threat ability would outshine Mahomes' arm talent and improvisational skills.

Eagles' Defense vs. Chiefs' Offense:
The Eagles boasted one of the league's most formidable defenses, while the Chiefs had an

explosive offense led by Mahomes and Kelce. The battle between these units was expected to be a key factor in determining the outcome of the game.

The Saquon Barkley Factor:

Barkley's presence in the Eagles' backfield added a new dimension to their offense. His ability to break tackles and gain yards after contact made him a player to watch. Many experts predicted that Barkley's performance could be a game-changer.

Coaching Battle:

The clash between Nick Sirianni and Andy Reid was a storyline in itself. Sirianni, a rising star in the coaching world, was up against the seasoned and highly respected Reid. Their contrasting coaching styles added intrigue to the matchup.

The Halftime Show:

Kendrick Lamar was set to headline the halftime show, adding an element of excitement beyond the game itself. Fans speculated about potential guest appearances and the cultural impact of Lamar's performance.

Expert Predictions

Analysts were divided on their predictions for the game. Some believed that the Eagles' balanced attack and suffocating defense would give them the edge. Others argued that Mahomes' brilliance and the Chiefs' playoff experience would be too much for the Eagles to handle.

Prominent analysts like Stephen A. Smith leaned toward the Eagles, citing their dominance throughout the season and the addition of Saquon Barkley as a key factor. On the other hand, former players like Tony Romo predicted a Chiefs victory, pointing to Mahomes' ability to perform in clutch situations.

Vegas oddsmakers had the game as a near toss-up, with a slight edge given to the Chiefs due to their recent Super Bowl success.

Final Preparations
The day before the Super Bowl, both teams held their final walkthroughs at the stadium. Players appeared focused and confident, knowing that all the hard work of the season had led to this moment.

As the sun set on the eve of Super Bowl LIX, fans and analysts alike braced themselves for an epic battle. The pre-game build-up had set the stage for a game that would be remembered for years to come. The only question remaining was which team would rise to the occasion and etch their names in NFL history.

Chapter 2: Game Day Highlights

Stadium Atmosphere and Opening Ceremonies

Super Bowl LIX kicked off with an electrifying atmosphere as fans from across the nation and around the world converged at Allegiant Stadium in Las Vegas. The state-of-the-art venue was transformed into a spectacle of color, energy, and anticipation as thousands of spectators took their seats, ready to witness the ultimate showdown between the Philadelphia Eagles and the Kansas City Chiefs.

The buzz around the stadium was palpable, with fans donning their team's colors, waving banners, and chanting in support of their respective teams. The streets surrounding the stadium were a hive of activity, filled with tailgating parties, live entertainment, and food vendors offering everything from classic hot dogs to gourmet delicacies. Las Vegas, known for its vibrant nightlife and entertainment scene, was the perfect backdrop for such a grand event.

Fan Energy and Pre-Game Festivities

As fans poured into the stadium, the atmosphere became even more electric. The roar of the crowd echoed through the venue as pre-game festivities commenced. Inside the stadium, giant screens displayed highlights from both teams' seasons, building anticipation for the battle that was about to unfold.

The NFL had gone all out to ensure that fans were treated to a memorable experience. A pre-game concert featuring chart-topping artists set the tone for the evening, with performances that had the crowd dancing and singing along. The energy was infectious, as fans of all ages reveled in the excitement of the biggest game of the year.

Outside the stadium, NFL Experience zones were set up, allowing fans to engage in interactive games, meet former players, and purchase exclusive Super Bowl merchandise. The atmosphere was a blend of sports fanaticism and entertainment, making it a true celebration of football culture.

Stadium Design and Crowd Energy

Allegiant Stadium, often referred to as "The Death Star" due to its sleek and futuristic design, was a marvel to behold. The retractable roof was closed, ensuring perfect weather conditions inside the venue. The stadium's massive LED screens and state-of-the-art sound system enhanced the visual and auditory experience for fans.

The seating was filled to capacity, with nearly 70,000 fans creating a sea of green and red, representing the Eagles and Chiefs respectively. Chants of "Fly, Eagles, Fly" and "Chiefs Kingdom" echoed throughout the stadium as fans rallied behind their teams. The excitement was palpable, with spectators on their feet, waving flags and cheering with unbridled enthusiasm.

Opening Ceremonies

The opening ceremonies were nothing short of spectacular. The NFL spared no expense in creating a visually stunning and emotionally charged pre-game show. The event began with a breathtaking flyover by the United States Air Force Thunderbirds, their jets painting the sky with vibrant trails of smoke as they soared over the stadium.

The national anthem, performed by a world-renowned singer, was a moment of unity and pride. As the final notes of "The Star-Spangled Banner" echoed through the stadium, fireworks lit up the sky, drawing thunderous applause from the crowd. The sight of players standing solemnly on the field, many with their hands over their hearts, was a powerful reminder of the significance of the moment.

A special tribute was also made to military personnel and first responders, with a heartfelt message of gratitude displayed on the stadium's giant screens. The crowd responded with a standing ovation, underscoring the deep respect and appreciation for those who serve the nation.

Player Introductions and Coin Toss

As the opening ceremonies concluded, it was time for player introductions. The stadium erupted in cheers as the Eagles and Chiefs took the field. Each player was individually announced, running through a tunnel of smoke and lights as they were greeted by the deafening roar of the crowd.

The energy was infectious, with players feeding off the excitement. Jalen Hurts and Patrick Mahomes received particularly loud ovations, as fans recognized the significance of the quarterback duel that was about to take place. The sight of both teams lining up on the field, poised and ready, was a powerful visual representation of the culmination of months of hard work and dedication.

The coin toss, a time-honored Super Bowl tradition, was conducted at midfield. Legendary former NFL players were invited to the field to perform the ceremonial toss, adding a touch of history to the moment. The Chiefs won the toss and chose to defer, giving the Eagles the first possession. The stage was set, and the excitement reached a fever pitch.

The Calm Before the Storm
As the teams huddled on the sidelines and prepared for kickoff, there was a brief moment of stillness. The crowd, momentarily hushed, seemed to collectively hold its breath in anticipation. Coaches gave final instructions, players adjusted their gear, and referees took their positions.

This was the calm before the storm—the last few seconds before the game that would crown the champion of Super Bowl LIX began. The energy was electric, the stakes were monumental, and everyone in the stadium knew they were about to witness history.

When the referee's whistle finally blew and the ball sailed through the air for the opening kickoff, Allegiant Stadium erupted in cheers. Super Bowl LIX was officially underway, and both the

Philadelphia Eagles and the Kansas City Chiefs were ready to leave everything on the field.

First Half Key Moments

The first half of Super Bowl LIX delivered a thrilling display of high-intensity football, filled with pivotal plays, strategic brilliance, and unforgettable moments. Fans at Allegiant Stadium and millions watching worldwide were treated to an epic contest between the Philadelphia Eagles and the Kansas City Chiefs as both teams fought fiercely to gain the upper hand. The stakes were high, and neither side was willing to back down.

Eagles Strike First

The Philadelphia Eagles wasted no time making their presence felt. After winning possession on the opening kickoff, Jalen Hurts led his team on a meticulously crafted drive down the field. The Eagles' offense looked unstoppable as Hurts showcased his precision passing and remarkable mobility.

Saquon Barkley played a crucial role in this early momentum, breaking tackles and picking up critical yards to keep the chains moving. On a crucial third-down play inside the red zone, Hurts connected with wide receiver A.J. Brown on a perfectly timed slant route for the game's first touchdown. The stadium erupted as Eagles fans celebrated their team's quick start.

The successful extra point made the score 7-0 in favor of the Eagles, setting the tone for what was shaping up to be an exhilarating game.

Chiefs Respond with Offensive Firepower
The Kansas City Chiefs, known for their explosive offense, wasted no time answering back. Patrick Mahomes, calm and collected, orchestrated a brilliant drive that highlighted his trademark creativity and accuracy. Utilizing a mix of short passes and quick handoffs to Isiah Pacheco, Mahomes kept the Eagles' defense on their heels.

A crucial third-down conversion to Travis Kelce kept the drive alive, and just a few plays later, Mahomes launched a beautifully arced pass to Kelce in the end zone for a touchdown. The connection between Mahomes and Kelce had been a cornerstone of the Chiefs' success throughout the season, and it continued to shine on the biggest stage.

With the extra point, the game was tied at 7-7, setting up an intense back-and-forth battle.

Defensive Stand-Offs and Strategic Plays

Both teams tightened up defensively after their initial scoring drives. The Eagles' front seven, led by Haason Reddick and Fletcher Cox, applied relentless pressure on Mahomes, forcing him to make hurried throws and limiting the Chiefs' offensive rhythm.

On the other side, Chris Jones and the Chiefs' defense stepped up their game, disrupting Hurts' passing lanes and containing Saquon Barkley. A crucial sack by Jones on a third-down play forced the Eagles to punt, giving the Chiefs a chance to seize momentum.

Despite the defensive dominance, both teams continued to showcase flashes of brilliance. Mahomes executed a dazzling 20-yard scramble to extend a drive, while Hurts responded with a stunning 40-yard bomb to DeVonta Smith that brought Eagles fans to their feet.

Turnovers and Momentum Shifts

As the first half progressed, turnovers became a defining factor. With the game tied at 10-10, the Eagles appeared poised to retake the lead. However, disaster struck when Hurts was stripped of the ball by Chiefs linebacker Nick Bolton. Bolton scooped up the fumble and sprinted 30 yards into the end zone for a defensive touchdown.

The momentum swung dramatically in favor of the Chiefs, who now led 17-10. The turnover silenced the Eagles' fans and ignited the Chiefs' sideline.

Undeterred, the Eagles regrouped. On their very next possession, Hurts led a determined drive, capped off by a spectacular 15-yard touchdown run where he juked past multiple defenders. The successful two-point conversion tied the game at 17-17, reigniting the crowd's energy.

Special Teams Impact

Special teams played a crucial role in the first half, with both teams executing key plays that impacted field position. The Eagles' punter delivered a perfectly placed kick that pinned the Chiefs inside their own 5-yard line, forcing Mahomes and the offense to start deep in their territory.

On the Chiefs' side, kicker Harrison Butker nailed a 50-yard field goal despite swirling winds inside the stadium, showcasing his composure and skill. These moments highlighted the importance of every phase of the game in a tightly contested Super Bowl.

Late-Quarter Drama

As the first half neared its conclusion, both teams ramped up their efforts to gain an edge before halftime. The Eagles managed to drive into Chiefs territory, but a crucial pass breakup by Kansas City's secondary on fourth down halted their progress.

Mahomes seized the opportunity, executing a rapid-fire drive with under two minutes left on the clock. A series of precise passes brought the Chiefs to the Eagles' 30-yard line. With just seconds remaining, Butker was called upon once again and delivered a clutch field goal to give the Chiefs a 20-17 lead heading into halftime.

Halftime Buzz and Analysis

The first half had been a rollercoaster of emotions, filled with spectacular plays, dramatic turnovers, and strategic brilliance from both teams. Fans and analysts alike were captivated by the intensity of the game.

The halftime show featuring Kendrick Lamar was eagerly anticipated, but discussions about the game dominated conversations in the stands and on social media. Analysts debated the impact of Hurts' fumble, Mahomes' composure under pressure, and the impressive performances of both defenses.

As the teams headed to their locker rooms to regroup and strategize, one thing was clear: Super Bowl LIX was living up to the hype. Both the Eagles and the Chiefs had proven their mettle, and the second half promised to be just as thrilling. Fans braced themselves for what was sure to be an unforgettable conclusion to a remarkable game.

Tactical Insights and Team Performance

Super Bowl LIX was a true testament to the strategic genius and adaptability of both the Philadelphia Eagles and the Kansas City Chiefs. Beyond the raw athleticism displayed on the field, it was a battle of minds between the coaching staff, who had meticulously prepared their teams for this high-stakes game. Both teams showcased tactical brilliance, innovative plays, and a deep understanding of the nuances of the sport.

Philadelphia Eagles' Offensive and Defensive Strategy

The Eagles entered the game with a well-crafted plan centered around their dynamic offense and aggressive defense. Head coach Nick Sirianni's tactical approach was evident from the first snap, as the Eagles utilized a balanced mix of passing and running plays to keep the Chiefs' defense guessing.

Offensive Strategy

Jalen Hurts was the linchpin of the Eagles' offensive scheme. His ability to seamlessly switch between passing and rushing plays kept the Chiefs' defense on their toes. The Eagles capitalized on Hurts' dual-threat capabilities by incorporating designed quarterback runs and read-option plays. These tactics allowed Hurts to exploit gaps in the Chiefs' defense and gain crucial yardage.

The offensive line played a pivotal role in the Eagles' success, providing Hurts with ample time to make decisions and creating running lanes for Saquon Barkley. The Eagles' receivers, led by A.J. Brown and DeVonta Smith, executed precise routes and made key catches to extend drives. Sirianni's decision to use quick, short passes helped neutralize the Chiefs' pass rush and maintain offensive rhythm.

Defensive Strategy

Defensively, the Eagles adopted a high-pressure approach, aiming to disrupt Patrick Mahomes' timing and force hurried throws. The front seven, anchored by Haason Reddick and Fletcher Cox, consistently collapsed the pocket and applied relentless pressure on Mahomes. This strategy was effective in limiting the Chiefs' explosive plays and forcing several third-and-long situations.

The secondary played tight coverage on the Chiefs' receivers, particularly Travis Kelce, who was double-teamed for much of the game. The Eagles' defensive backs showcased exceptional discipline and communication, preventing breakdowns in coverage and minimizing big gains.

Kansas City Chiefs' Offensive and Defensive Strategy

Head coach Andy Reid, known for his offensive brilliance, crafted a game plan that emphasized creativity and adaptability. The Chiefs relied on Mahomes' ability to extend plays and his chemistry with key targets to dismantle the Eagles' defense.

Offensive Strategy

Mahomes' improvisational skills were on full display throughout the game. The Chiefs utilized a spread offense, spreading out the Eagles' defenders and creating mismatches in coverage. Quick screens and slant routes allowed Mahomes to get the ball out quickly and neutralize the Eagles' pass rush.

Reid's play-calling was a masterclass in deception. The Chiefs frequently employed pre-snap motion and misdirection plays to confuse the Eagles' defense. One notable play involved a jet sweep fake that drew the defense to one side, allowing Mahomes to connect with a wide-open Marquez Valdes-Scantling for a significant gain.

Travis Kelce remained a focal point of the offense despite the Eagles' double coverage. His ability to find soft spots in the defense and make contested catches was instrumental in sustaining drives. Isiah Pacheco's powerful running added a crucial dimension to the Chiefs' offense, keeping the Eagles' defense honest.

Defensive Strategy

Defensively, the Chiefs adopted a bend-but-don't-break approach. Defensive coordinator Steve Spagnuolo dialed up creative blitz packages to disrupt Hurts' rhythm and force mistakes. Chris Jones was a dominant force on the defensive line, consistently penetrating the Eagles' backfield and making key tackles.

The Chiefs' secondary played a crucial role in containing the Eagles' explosive passing game. They employed zone coverage schemes that forced Hurts to make difficult throws into tight windows. Rookie cornerback Trent McDuffie delivered an impressive performance, breaking up several passes and demonstrating poise under pressure.

Spagnuolo's decision to switch between man and zone coverage kept the Eagles' offense off balance and prevented them from establishing a consistent rhythm.

Key Tactical Adjustments

Both teams made critical adjustments as the game progressed.

Eagles' Adjustments: After struggling with turnovers and defensive pressure, the Eagles focused on quick, high-percentage passes to regain momentum. They also increased their use of screen plays to counter the Chiefs' aggressive blitzes. Defensively, the Eagles shifted to a more conservative approach, prioritizing containment rather than all-out pressure.

Chiefs' Adjustments: Recognizing the need to neutralize Hurts' rushing ability, the Chiefs adjusted their defensive front, deploying a spy to monitor his movements. Offensively, they incorporated more play-action passes and rollouts to create time and space for Mahomes.

Special Teams and Tactical Impact

Special teams played a crucial tactical role in the game. The Chiefs' decision to attempt a surprise onside kick in the second quarter was a bold move that nearly paid off. Meanwhile, the Eagles' punting strategy consistently pinned the Chiefs deep in their territory, forcing them to start drives with poor field position.

Coaching Brilliance

The tactical insights and decisions made by Nick Sirianni and Andy Reid were a testament to their coaching brilliance. Sirianni's aggressive play-calling and trust in Hurts showcased his confidence in the team's offensive capabilities. Reid's ability to adapt and exploit weaknesses in the Eagles' defense demonstrated his mastery of in-game adjustments.

Both coaches displayed remarkable composure and leadership, guiding their teams through the highs and lows of the game. Their tactical genius was evident in every play, making Super Bowl LIX a true chess match on the gridiron.

The tactical battle between the Eagles and the Chiefs was a defining aspect of Super Bowl LIX. Both teams executed their game plans with precision, showcasing the strategic depth and adaptability required to compete at the highest level. The first half set the stage for an unforgettable contest, and the tactical brilliance displayed by both teams ensured that fans were treated to a spectacle of football excellence.

Chapter 3: The Second Half and Victory

Turning Points of the Game

The second half of Super Bowl LIX unfolded with dramatic twists and thrilling moments that defined the championship. Both the Philadelphia Eagles and the Kansas City Chiefs returned from halftime reinvigorated, knowing that this was their chance to cement a place in football history. The turning points in this half were pivotal, not only for the scoreline but for the morale and momentum of the teams.

Halftime Adjustments and Fresh Energy

The Chiefs entered the second half trailing by three points, but they had momentum on their side after a clutch field goal just before halftime. Head coach Andy Reid was known for his ability to make effective halftime adjustments, and this game was no exception. Reid focused on giving Patrick Mahomes quicker options to avoid the relentless Eagles pass rush and emphasized more creative run plays to balance the offense.

Nick Sirianni, on the other hand, urged the Eagles to maintain their aggressive approach while reducing turnovers and tightening up defensive coverage. His message to the team was simple: "Stay disciplined and finish strong."

The atmosphere was electric as both teams took the field. Fans braced themselves for what promised to be a second half filled with intensity and unpredictability.

Mahomes' Comeback Heroics
Early in the third quarter, disaster appeared to strike for the Chiefs when Patrick Mahomes was tackled awkwardly on a scramble attempt. Limping off the field, Mahomes grimaced in pain, raising concerns about his ability to continue. However, in a testament to his resilience and leadership, Mahomes returned to the field just a few plays later, determined to lead his team.

With Mahomes back in action, the Chiefs' offense found its rhythm. On a crucial third-and-long play, Mahomes escaped pressure and delivered a stunning 30-yard pass to Travis Kelce, reigniting the Chiefs' momentum. The drive culminated in a perfectly executed screen pass to Isiah Pacheco, who sprinted into the end zone for a touchdown. The Chiefs had reclaimed the lead, and the energy on their sideline was palpable.

Eagles' Counterattack
The Eagles, now trailing, knew they had to respond quickly. Jalen Hurts demonstrated remarkable composure as he led a methodical drive down the field. Saquon Barkley continued to be a key factor, breaking tackles and gaining significant yards to keep the drive alive.

On a crucial fourth-and-goal situation, Sirianni made a bold decision to go for it rather than settle for a field goal. Hurts took the snap and powered his way into the end zone with a quarterback sneak, tying the game once again. The Eagles' sideline erupted in celebration, and it was clear that this game was far from over.

Defensive Standoff and Key Turnover
As the fourth quarter began, both defenses tightened up, recognizing the magnitude of the moment. The Eagles' front seven, led by Haason Reddick, relentlessly pressured Mahomes, while the Chiefs' secondary delivered crucial pass breakups to thwart Hurts' attempts downfield.

The turning point came midway through the fourth quarter when the Eagles, driving deep into Chiefs territory, committed a costly turnover. Hurts, under heavy pressure, attempted a pass to A.J. Brown, but Chiefs linebacker Nick Bolton read the play perfectly and intercepted the ball. Bolton's return to midfield shifted momentum squarely in favor of Kansas City.

Game-Winning Drive

With just minutes left on the clock, Mahomes orchestrated what would become one of the most memorable drives in Super Bowl history. The Chiefs' offense executed flawlessly, blending quick passes and strategic runs to chew up the clock and march down the field.

One of the defining moments of the drive was a spectacular 20-yard completion to Travis Kelce, who made a leaping catch despite tight coverage. Mahomes then followed up with a perfectly timed screen pass to Jerick McKinnon, who smartly slid to keep the clock running rather than scoring immediately.

With seconds remaining, Harrison Butker was called upon to deliver the game-winning field goal. The stadium fell silent as Butker lined up for the kick. With nerves of steel, he sent the ball soaring through the uprights, giving the Chiefs a three-point lead.

Final Attempt by the Eagles

With just seconds left on the clock, the Eagles had one last chance to pull off a miracle. Hurts launched a desperate Hail Mary pass from his own 40-yard line, but the ball fell incomplete as time expired. The Chiefs' sideline erupted in jubilation as they secured a hard-fought victory.

Post-Game Reactions and Analysis

The Chiefs' victory was a testament to their resilience, adaptability, and championship pedigree. Patrick Mahomes' heroic performance earned him the Super Bowl MVP award, solidifying his status as one of the greatest quarterbacks of his generation. Andy Reid's tactical brilliance and calm leadership were widely praised.

On the Eagles' side, there was heartbreak but also pride. Jalen Hurts' remarkable performance and leadership were undeniable, and Nick Sirianni commended his team's effort and determination. Despite the loss, the Eagles had proven themselves as one of the league's elite teams.

The turning points of Super Bowl LIX showcased the essence of championship football — resilience, adaptability, and clutch performances under immense pressure. Both teams left everything on the field, but it was the Chiefs who emerged victorious in a game that will be remembered for its drama, intensity, and unforgettable moments. Fans and analysts alike would discuss the strategic moves, game-changing plays, and remarkable performances for years to come.

Game-Changing Plays

Super Bowl LIX was a game defined by pivotal moments that shifted momentum and determined the outcome of the championship. From spectacular touchdowns to clutch defensive stops, the game featured a series of plays that showcased the brilliance, determination, and adaptability of both teams. These game-changing plays were the heartbeat of the second half and ultimately decided the fate of the Lombardi Trophy.

Mahomes' Stunning 30-Yard Pass to Travis Kelce

One of the most crucial plays in the second half occurred early in the third quarter. Facing a daunting third-and-long situation, Patrick Mahomes, despite battling an ankle injury, displayed remarkable composure under pressure. Escaping a collapsing pocket, Mahomes launched a perfectly arched 30-yard pass downfield to his favorite target, Travis Kelce.

Kelce, tightly covered by two Eagles defenders, made an acrobatic catch, dragging his feet in bounds to secure the completion. This play not only extended the Chiefs' drive but also reignited their momentum and confidence. The Chiefs capitalized on this pivotal moment by pp
scoring a touchdown that brought them back into contention.

Jalen Hurts' Fourth-and-Goal Touchdown Sneak
With the Chiefs taking the lead, the Eagles found themselves in a critical situation midway through the third quarter. They faced a fourth-and-goal from the two-yard line. Head coach Nick Sirianni made the bold decision to go for it, trusting his offense to deliver in the high-pressure moment.

Jalen Hurts took the snap and, with the help of a strong push from his offensive line, muscled his way into the end zone for a touchdown. This gutsy play not only tied the game but also demonstrated the Eagles' resilience and aggressive mindset. The decision to go for it on fourth down became a defining moment for the Eagles' championship aspirations.

Nick Bolton's Game-Changing Interception

As the fourth quarter began, the game was on a knife's edge, with both teams battling for control. The Eagles were driving deep into Chiefs territory, looking to regain the lead. Jalen Hurts dropped back to pass, targeting A.J. Brown on a slant route.

However, Chiefs linebacker Nick Bolton read the play perfectly. Bolton, showing incredible anticipation and agility, stepped in front of the pass and intercepted it. What made this play even more remarkable was Bolton's ability to return the interception to midfield, giving the Chiefs excellent field position.

This turnover proved to be a turning point in the game, shifting momentum firmly in favor of Kansas City and setting up a crucial scoring drive.

Jerick McKinnon's Strategic Slide

With less than two minutes left in the game and the score tied, the Chiefs found themselves deep in Eagles territory. On a second-and-goal play, Jerick McKinnon took a handoff and had a clear path to the end zone. However, instead of scoring, McKinnon made a smart and selfless decision — he slid down just short of the goal line.

This play was a masterclass in game awareness. By not scoring, McKinnon ensured that the Chiefs could run down the clock, leaving the Eagles with no time to mount a comeback. It was a moment of discipline and strategic brilliance that highlighted the Chiefs' commitment to winning as a team.

Harrison Butker's Game-Winning Field Goal
With just seconds left on the clock, the Chiefs called upon their reliable kicker, Harrison Butker, to seal the victory. Butker had missed a field goal earlier in the game, but he showed remarkable poise as he lined up for the 38-yard attempt.

The stadium fell silent as Butker took his steps and delivered a flawless kick that sailed through the uprights. The Chiefs' sideline erupted in celebration as Butker's field goal gave them a three-point lead. It was a clutch moment that cemented his legacy as a hero of Super Bowl LIX.

Eagles' Final Hail Mary Attempt
With only a few seconds remaining, the Eagles had one last chance to pull off a miracle. Jalen Hurts took the snap and scrambled to create space for a desperate Hail Mary attempt. Under heavy pressure, Hurts launched the ball downfield, aiming for the end zone.

As the ball sailed through the air, fans held their breath. However, it fell incomplete, landing harmlessly on the turf. The Chiefs' defenders celebrated as time expired, knowing they had secured a hard-fought victory.

Impact of Game-Changing Plays on Momentum

These game-changing plays were the defining moments of Super Bowl LIX. Each play had a ripple effect, influencing the strategies, morale, and performance of both teams. Mahomes' deep pass to Kelce ignited the Chiefs' offense, while Hurts' fourth-down touchdown showcased the Eagles' tenacity.

Nick Bolton's interception shifted the momentum in favor of the Chiefs, and McKinnon's strategic slide demonstrated exceptional game awareness. Harrison Butker's game-winning field goal was the final piece of the puzzle, sealing a victory that will be remembered for years to come.

Super Bowl LIX was a masterclass in football drama, with game-changing plays that highlighted the skill, strategy, and determination of both teams. These moments not only defined the game but also etched themselves into the memories of fans around the world. The Chiefs' victory was a testament to their ability to capitalize on these critical plays and emerge as champions on the grandest stage of all.

Final Score and Eagles' Triumph

In a commanding performance, the Philadelphia Eagles secured their second Super Bowl title by defeating the Kansas City Chiefs 40-22 in Super Bowl LIX, held at the Caesars Superdome in New Orleans.

The Eagles established dominance early, building a 24-0 lead by halftime, thanks to a combination of offensive efficiency and defensive prowess. Quarterback Jalen Hurts delivered an exceptional performance, completing 17 of 22 passes for 221 yards and two touchdowns, alongside a rushing touchdown. His efforts earned him the Super Bowl MVP award.

The defense played a pivotal role, forcing two first-half interceptions that stymied the Chiefs' offense. Linebacker Nick Bolton's interception return for a touchdown was a highlight, contributing to the early lead.

Despite a late surge by the Chiefs, including a 50-yard touchdown pass to Xavier Worthy, the Eagles maintained control throughout the game. This victory prevented the Chiefs from achieving a third consecutive Super Bowl win and solidified the Eagles' status as one of the NFL's premier teams.

The triumph was celebrated by fans and analysts alike, marking a significant milestone in the Eagles' franchise history.

Super Bowl LIX concluded with a decisive 40-22 victory for the Philadelphia Eagles over the Kansas City Chiefs. The game showcased the Eagles' dominance on both sides of the ball and solidified their place as one of the most formidable teams in recent NFL history. Their triumph was built on a combination of tactical brilliance, key player performances, and a relentless defensive approach.

Eagles' First-Half Dominance

The tone for the Eagles' victory was set in the first half, where they stormed to a commanding 24-0 lead. Quarterback Jalen Hurts orchestrated an efficient offensive strategy, making precise throws and leading scoring drives with confidence. His composure and decision-making were unmatched, keeping the Chiefs' defense on its heels.

Hurts' connection with wide receiver A.J. Brown was particularly impactful. Brown made critical catches that extended drives and put the Eagles in scoring position. The offensive line also played a vital role, providing Hurts with the protection needed to execute plays seamlessly.

On the defensive side, the Eagles were relentless. Linebacker Nick Bolton's interception, returned for a touchdown, was one of the game's defining moments. The Eagles' defense continually applied pressure on Chiefs quarterback Patrick Mahomes, forcing him to make hurried throws and limiting his ability to create plays.

Chiefs' Attempted Comeback

Despite the Eagles' first-half dominance, the Chiefs mounted a spirited comeback attempt in the second half. Mahomes showcased his trademark resilience, engineering a series of impressive drives. One of the most memorable moments was a 50-yard touchdown pass to Xavier Worthy, which energized the Chiefs and narrowed the Eagles' lead.

The Chiefs' defense also stepped up, making crucial stops and forcing turnovers that gave their offense opportunities to close the gap. However, the Eagles' defense remained disciplined and thwarted several key plays.

Jalen Hurts' MVP Performance

Hurts' leadership and performance earned him the Super Bowl MVP award. He completed 17 of 22 passes for 221 yards and two touchdowns, in addition to scoring a rushing touchdown. His ability to make smart decisions under pressure and execute game-changing plays was instrumental in the Eagles' victory.

Hurts' dual-threat capability made him a constant threat to the Chiefs' defense. Whether through precise passing or strategic runs, he consistently found ways to keep the Eagles' offense moving down the field.

Clutch Defensive Stops

The Eagles' defense played a pivotal role in securing the victory. Key tackles, deflections, and disciplined coverage prevented the Chiefs from gaining the momentum they needed for a complete comeback. The defensive line's ability to disrupt Mahomes' rhythm was particularly notable.

The Eagles' defense made a critical stand in the fourth quarter when the Chiefs were driving deep into Eagles territory. A perfectly timed blitz forced an incomplete pass on fourth down, effectively sealing the game for the Eagles.

The Game-Winning Drive and Butker's Missed Opportunity

Late in the fourth quarter, the Eagles orchestrated a methodical drive that consumed valuable time off the clock. They relied on a balanced mix of runs and short passes to move down the field and set up a crucial scoring opportunity.

Harrison Butker, known for his clutch kicking abilities, had a chance to put the Chiefs back in contention with a long field goal. However, his attempt sailed wide, effectively ending the Chiefs' hopes and allowing the Eagles to run out the clock.

Celebrations and Legacy

As the final seconds ticked away, the Eagles' sidelines erupted in celebration. Players, coaches, and fans rejoiced in the realization that they had captured the Super Bowl LIX title. The victory was a testament to the team's hard work, determination, and unwavering belief in their abilities.

The Eagles' triumph not only marked their second Super Bowl win but also prevented the Chiefs from securing a third consecutive championship. It was a defining moment in the franchise's history and a proud day for Eagles fans everywhere.

The final score of 40-22 highlighted the Eagles' dominance and resilience throughout the game. Their ability to execute game-winning plays, maintain composure under pressure, and make critical defensive stops secured their well-deserved victory. Super Bowl LIX will be remembered as a game where the Eagles soared to new heights, cementing their legacy in NFL history.

Chapter 4: Standout Performances and Records

Jalen Hurts' MVP Moment

In Super Bowl LIX, Jalen Hurts delivered a performance that will be remembered as one of the most remarkable in the history of the championship game. His outstanding leadership, dynamic playmaking abilities, and composure under pressure earned him the coveted Super Bowl MVP award. Hurts' ability to elevate his game on the grandest stage not only secured a victory for the Philadelphia Eagles but also cemented his reputation as one of the NFL's elite quarterbacks.

A Commanding Performance

Hurts' MVP moment was defined by his exceptional statistics and decision-making throughout the game. He completed 17 of 22 pass attempts for 221 yards and two touchdowns. His precision passing kept the Eagles' offense moving efficiently and prevented the Kansas City Chiefs' defense from gaining any significant momentum.

One of Hurts' most memorable plays came in the second quarter when he connected with wide receiver A.J. Brown for a 45-yard touchdown. The perfectly placed pass demonstrated his deep-ball accuracy and ability to capitalize on defensive mismatches. The play electrified the Eagles' fans and gave the team a comfortable lead.

Dual-Threat Brilliance

In addition to his impressive passing performance, Hurts showcased his prowess as a dual-threat quarterback. His ability to read defensive formations and make the right decision between passing and running was crucial to the Eagles' offensive success. Hurts rushed for 58 yards and a touchdown, using his speed and agility to escape pressure and gain critical yards when the pocket collapsed.

His rushing touchdown in the third quarter was a testament to his toughness and determination. On a designed quarterback run, Hurts powered through defenders to reach the end zone, igniting celebrations on the Eagles' sidelines. This play not only extended the Eagles' lead but also demoralized the Chiefs' defense.

Leadership and Poise Under Pressure

Perhaps one of the most impressive aspects of Hurts' performance was his ability to remain calm and composed under pressure. As the Chiefs mounted a second-half comeback, Hurts kept his offense focused and motivated. His leadership was evident in the way he communicated with his teammates, adjusted plays at the line of scrimmage, and made critical decisions during high-pressure situations.

Hurts' poise was particularly evident during the Eagles' game-sealing drive in the fourth quarter. With the Chiefs closing in, Hurts orchestrated a methodical series of plays that chewed up valuable time on the clock and set up a crucial field goal attempt. His ability to manage the game in such a tense moment highlighted his maturity and football IQ.

Earning the MVP Award

Hurts' performance was nothing short of spectacular, and it was no surprise when he was named Super Bowl MVP. The award was a recognition of his complete command of the game and his pivotal role in the Eagles' victory. Hurts became the first Eagles quarterback to win the award since Nick Foles in Super Bowl LII, joining an elite group of players who have achieved this honor.

During the post-game ceremony, Hurts stood on the podium with a humble smile as he accepted the MVP trophy. In his speech, he credited his teammates, coaches, and the Eagles' fans for their unwavering support. His words reflected the humility and gratitude that have become hallmarks of his character.

A Legacy-Defining Moment
Jalen Hurts' MVP moment in Super Bowl LIX was more than just a personal achievement; it was a defining chapter in his career and a milestone for the Eagles' franchise. His ability to rise to the occasion on the biggest stage demonstrated his status as a true leader and a generational talent.

The victory and Hurts' MVP performance will undoubtedly be etched in the memories of Eagles fans for years to come. His journey from a promising young quarterback to a Super Bowl champion and MVP is a testament to his hard work, resilience, and unwavering belief in himself.

As the confetti rained down and the celebrations continued long into the night, one thing was clear: Jalen Hurts had cemented his place in NFL history, and Super Bowl LIX would forever be remembered as the stage where he shined brightest.

Saquon Barkley's Contributions

In Super Bowl LIX, while the Philadelphia Eagles' 40-22 victory over the Kansas City Chiefs was highlighted by quarterback Jalen Hurts' MVP performance, running back Saquon Barkley also made significant contributions throughout the season and in the championship game.

Season Milestones Leading to the Super Bowl

Barkley's impact was most evident during the regular season and playoffs, where he amassed a record-breaking total of 2,504 rushing yards, surpassing Terrell Davis's previous single-season record. His 18 touchdowns were instrumental in securing the Eagles' path to the Super Bowl.

Super Bowl LIX Performance

In the Super Bowl, Barkley faced a formidable Chiefs defense that focused on limiting his effectiveness. Despite their efforts, he managed to contribute 57 rushing yards, providing the Eagles with crucial yardage and maintaining offensive balance.

Leadership and Locker Room Presence

Beyond his on-field performance, Barkley's leadership was evident in the locker room celebrations following the victory. He led the jubilant atmosphere, sharing moments with teammates and team owner Jeffrey Lurie, highlighting his integral role within the team dynamic.

Reflecting on the Journey

Reflecting on his journey, Barkley expressed deep gratitude towards his former team, the New York Giants, and their fans. He acknowledged the support he received during his six seasons with the Giants and cherished the opportunity to hold the Vince Lombardi Trophy with the Eagles.

In summary, while Saquon Barkley's statistical contributions in Super Bowl LIX were modest, his overall impact on the Eagles' championship season was profound. His record-breaking rushing performance throughout the season and his leadership both on and off the field were pivotal in the Eagles' successful campaign.

A Testament to Resilience and Growth

Barkley's journey to Super Bowl LIX was one marked by resilience and personal growth. Having endured injuries and a challenging tenure with the

New York Giants, Barkley emerged stronger, showing incredible tenacity and adaptability. His decision to join the Eagles in pursuit of a championship proved to be a game-changing move for both him and the franchise.

During the postseason, Barkley demonstrated his ability to perform in high-pressure situations. His explosive runs and ability to break through defensive lines often swung the momentum in favor of the Eagles. His versatility as both a rusher and a pass-catcher added depth to the Eagles' offensive playbook, making him a crucial weapon for head coach Nick Sirianni.

Impact Beyond Statistics

While Barkley's rushing yards in Super Bowl LIX may not have been record-breaking, his presence on the field drew significant attention from the Chiefs' defense. This attention created opportunities for other offensive players, such as A.J. Brown and DeVonta Smith, to thrive. Barkley's ability to execute blocks and provide pass protection also contributed to Jalen Hurts' success in the pocket.

Moreover, Barkley's leadership extended beyond the field. His positive attitude and motivational speeches in the locker room inspired his teammates throughout the season. Younger players often looked up to him for guidance and advice, further solidifying his role as a veteran leader within the team.

Post-Game Reflections

After the Eagles' triumph, Barkley expressed his gratitude to the organization, his teammates, and the fans. In post-game interviews, he emphasized the importance of teamwork and resilience in achieving success. Barkley also reflected on his journey from the Giants to the Eagles, acknowledging the challenges he had faced and the joy of finally lifting the Vince Lombardi Trophy.

"It's been a long journey, but every moment was worth it," Barkley said. "This team believed in me, and I believed in them. To stand here as a champion with these guys is a dream come true."

Legacy and Future Prospects

Barkley's contributions to the Eagles' championship season will be remembered as a turning point in his career. His ability to overcome adversity and play a pivotal role in the team's success highlighted his value as one of the league's premier running backs. The Super Bowl victory not only cemented his legacy but also opened up new possibilities for his future with the Eagles.

As the team looks ahead to future seasons, Barkley's experience and leadership will undoubtedly remain invaluable. His journey from a promising rookie with the Giants to a Super Bowl champion with the Eagles is a testament to his determination, skill, and unwavering commitment to excellence.

Key Defensive Players and Historical Achievements

In Super Bowl LIX, the Philadelphia Eagles and Kansas City Chiefs both showcased exceptional defensive units that played a critical role throughout the game and during the season leading up to it. While offensive plays often grab headlines, it was the defensive efforts that set the stage for key moments, shifted momentum, and ultimately shaped the outcome of the game. This chapter delves into the standout defensive players, their significant contributions, and the historical milestones achieved during this championship showdown.

Eagles' Dominant Defensive Line

The Eagles' defense was a force to be reckoned with throughout the season, leading the NFL in sacks and dominating opposing offensive lines. The team's defensive line was a standout group, anchored by seasoned veterans and rising stars who made their presence felt in Super Bowl LIX.

Haason Reddick: A Defensive Powerhouse

Haason Reddick emerged as one of the most formidable pass rushers for the Eagles. His explosive speed and relentless pursuit of the quarterback were instrumental in disrupting the Chiefs' offensive rhythm. During the Super Bowl, Reddick recorded multiple pressures and a crucial sack in the third quarter that shifted momentum in favor of the Eagles. His performance cemented his reputation as one of the league's top edge rushers.

Fletcher Cox: The Veteran Leader

Fletcher Cox, a seasoned defensive tackle and key leader for the Eagles, showcased his experience and skill on the grandest stage. His ability to collapse the pocket and stop the run made life difficult for the Chiefs' offensive line. Cox's leadership and veteran presence were invaluable in rallying the defensive unit during critical moments of the game.

Darius Slay: The Shutdown Cornerback

Darius Slay, known for his ability to lock down top receivers, played a pivotal role in containing the Chiefs' explosive passing game. His keen instincts and tight coverage limited the production of the Chiefs' star wideouts. Slay's contributions in the secondary were essential in maintaining the Eagles' defensive dominance.

Chiefs' Resilient Defense

Despite the Eagles' high-powered offense, the Chiefs' defense demonstrated resilience and adaptability throughout the game. They managed to force key turnovers and keep the game competitive well into the second half.

Chris Jones: A Defensive Juggernaut

Chris Jones, one of the league's premier defensive linemen, was a standout performer for the Chiefs. His strength and ability to penetrate the Eagles' offensive line made him a constant threat. Jones recorded several tackles for loss and provided much-needed pressure on Jalen Hurts, forcing hurried throws and disrupting the Eagles' offensive flow.

Nick Bolton: The Emerging Star

Nick Bolton, a rising star at linebacker, showcased his athleticism and playmaking ability during the Super Bowl. Bolton's ability to read plays and react quickly allowed him to make crucial stops and limit the Eagles' gains on the ground. His leadership in the middle of the field was a key factor in the Chiefs' defensive efforts.

L'Jarius Sneed: Defensive Back Excellence

L'Jarius Sneed played a vital role in the Chiefs' secondary, using his speed and coverage skills to contain the Eagles' dynamic receiving corps. Sneed's ability to anticipate routes and disrupt passing plays provided a critical defensive edge for the Chiefs.

Historical Achievements and Milestones

Super Bowl LIX was not just about individual performances; it was also a game that saw significant historical achievements and milestones on the defensive front.

Eagles Set Sack Records

The Eagles' defense set a franchise record for sacks during the season, with over 70 recorded by the end of the regular season. Their dominant pass rush was a defining characteristic of their success and highlighted their ability to pressure opposing quarterbacks consistently.

Turnover Battle and Key Defensive Plays

Both teams demonstrated the importance of turnovers in shaping the game. The Eagles forced a crucial fumble in the third quarter that led to a pivotal touchdown, while the Chiefs managed to intercept Hurts early in the game, temporarily halting the Eagles' offensive momentum.

Defensive MVP Consideration

While Jalen Hurts ultimately won the Super Bowl MVP award, several defensive players were in contention for the honor due to their impactful performances. Haason Reddick and Chris Jones, in particular, were recognized for their game-changing plays and leadership on the field.

Legacy of Defensive Greatness

Super Bowl LIX will be remembered not only for the offensive fireworks but also for the incredible defensive performances that defined key moments of the game. The contributions of players like Haason Reddick, Fletcher Cox, Chris Jones, and Nick Bolton underscored the importance of a strong defensive presence in achieving championship success.

As analysts and fans reflect on the game, the defensive battles and historical achievements will stand as a testament to the importance of defense in football. These players' efforts will be etched in Super Bowl history, serving as an inspiration for future generations of defensive stars.

Chapter 5: The Halftime Show and Cultural Impact

Kendrick Lamar's Performance Highlights

In the grand spectacle of Super Bowl LIX, held on February 9, 2025, at the Caesars Superdome in New Orleans, the halftime show emerged as a cultural milestone, headlined by the acclaimed rapper Kendrick Lamar. This performance not only showcased Lamar's artistic prowess but also underscored significant cultural themes, leaving an indelible mark on the event's history.

A Historic Moment in Hip-Hop

Kendrick Lamar's selection as the halftime performer was historic, marking the first time a solo rapper headlined the Super Bowl halftime show. This choice signified the NFL's recognition of hip-hop's profound influence on American culture and its global reach. Lamar, known for his intricate lyrics and thought-provoking themes, was an apt choice to represent the genre on such a prestigious platform.

Performance Highlights

The halftime show commenced with a dynamic entrance, as Lamar and his ensemble emerged from a 1980s Buick Regal, a nod to his roots and the cultural symbolism of the vehicle. The stage design, reminiscent of a giant PlayStation controller, added a contemporary and nostalgic touch, resonating with a broad audience.

The setlist was a curated blend of Lamar's hits and recent tracks, including:

"Bodies"
"Squabble Up"
"HUMBLE."
"DNA."
"Euphoria"
"Man at the Garden"
"Peekaboo"
"Luther" (featuring SZA)
"All the Stars" (featuring SZA)
"Not Like Us"
"TV Off" (with Mustard)

A standout moment was the performance of "Not Like Us," a track widely interpreted as a critique of fellow rapper Drake. This choice was bold, bringing the intricacies of hip-hop rivalries to a mainstream audience. Adding to the spectacle, tennis icon

Serena Williams made a brief yet memorable appearance, performing the Crip walk during this song, which became a viral sensation.

The show also featured appearances by actor Samuel L. Jackson, portraying Uncle Sam, and singer SZA, who joined Lamar for their collaborative tracks, enhancing the performance's depth and appeal.

Cultural Impact and Reception

Lamar's performance was lauded for its artistic depth and cultural commentary. By choosing to highlight themes of identity, rivalry, and societal issues, he deviated from the typical halftime show formula, offering a presentation that was both entertaining and thought-provoking. The inclusion of politically charged imagery and the deliberate song selection sparked discussions about the role of art in reflecting and challenging societal norms.

Critics noted that while the performance was less overtly political than some of Lamar's previous work, it still conveyed powerful messages through symbolism and narrative. The portrayal of Uncle Sam by Samuel L. Jackson and the patriotic color schemes used by dancers subtly addressed themes of American identity and critique.

Kendrick Lamar's halftime show at Super Bowl LIX was a landmark event that transcended the typical boundaries of sports entertainment. It highlighted the evolving landscape of mainstream performances, where artists can infuse their work with meaningful commentary while captivating a diverse audience. Lamar's ability to blend artistry with cultural critique ensured that his performance would be remembered as a significant moment in Super Bowl history.

Special Guest Appearances

One of the most anticipated elements of any Super Bowl halftime show is the possibility of surprise guest appearances, and Super Bowl LIX did not disappoint. Kendrick Lamar's electrifying performance was elevated by the presence of several high-profile celebrities who brought their unique flair to the stage. These special guests not only added to the visual and musical spectacle but also underscored the cultural and artistic significance of the event.

Serena Williams: A Show-Stopping Performance
Tennis legend Serena Williams made an unexpected and memorable appearance during Lamar's performance of "Not Like Us." Williams, known for her unparalleled achievements on the tennis court,

surprised the audience by joining the dancers on stage. Her confident moves, including the iconic Crip Walk, instantly went viral on social media, capturing the attention of fans and media alike.

Serena's appearance was more than just a dance moment; it was a symbol of the intersection between sports and entertainment, blending the worlds of athletics and music in a way that resonated with viewers. Her participation underscored the theme of empowerment and cultural pride that ran throughout Lamar's performance.

SZA: A Vocal Powerhouse

Singer-songwriter SZA, one of Kendrick Lamar's frequent collaborators, graced the stage to perform their hit songs "All the Stars" and "Luther." Her soulful voice added depth and emotion to the performance, creating a captivating contrast to Lamar's dynamic delivery.

Dressed in a stunning silver ensemble that shimmered under the stadium lights, SZA captivated the audience with her powerful vocals and commanding stage presence. Her chemistry with Lamar was palpable, and their joint performance was hailed as one of the highlights of the halftime show.

Samuel L. Jackson: The Patriotic Uncle Sam

Another surprise guest was Hollywood icon Samuel L. Jackson, who took on the role of a modern-day Uncle Sam. Dressed in a red, white, and blue outfit complete with a top hat, Jackson delivered a powerful monologue that blended elements of spoken word poetry and political commentary.

His presence added a theatrical element to the show, and his commanding voice captivated the audience as he spoke about themes of justice, freedom, and unity. The inclusion of Jackson's monologue was a bold artistic choice that added a layer of social commentary to the performance.

Mustard: The Beat Master

Renowned producer and DJ Mustard also made a guest appearance during Lamar's set. Known for his signature West Coast beats, Mustard brought an infectious energy to the stage, hyping up the crowd and adding a fresh, modern vibe to the performance.

His collaboration with Lamar on "TV Off" was a high-energy moment that had the entire stadium on its feet. Mustard's presence highlighted Lamar's ability to seamlessly blend different musical styles and bring together artists from diverse genres.

The Impact of Guest Appearances

The inclusion of these special guests added layers of excitement and cultural significance to the Super Bowl LIX halftime show. Each guest brought their unique talents and perspectives, creating a multifaceted performance that appealed to a wide audience.

Serena Williams' unexpected dance moves, SZA's soulful vocals, Samuel L. Jackson's powerful monologue, and Mustard's energetic beats all contributed to a show that was both entertaining and thought-provoking. These appearances underscored the collaborative nature of the music industry and highlighted Lamar's ability to curate a performance that celebrated diversity and unity.

A Lasting Impression

The guest appearances during Kendrick Lamar's halftime show will be remembered as a defining feature of Super Bowl LIX. They elevated the performance from a musical set to a cultural event that celebrated artistry, activism, and collaboration.

As fans and critics reflect on the show, it is clear that these special guests played a crucial role in creating a memorable and impactful halftime experience. Their contributions added depth and variety to the performance, ensuring that it will be remembered as one of the most iconic halftime shows in Super Bowl history.

Social and Cultural Significance

Super Bowl LIX was not just a sporting event; it was a cultural phenomenon that brought together millions of people across different backgrounds. Beyond the thrilling game and spectacular halftime show, the event highlighted broader social themes, celebrated diversity, and reinforced the influence of sports and entertainment on societal values. Kendrick Lamar's halftime performance, guest appearances, and even the narratives surrounding the teams reflected and contributed to these cultural conversations.

A Celebration of Diversity and Representation

One of the most significant aspects of Super Bowl LIX was its celebration of diversity. Kendrick Lamar's role as the halftime headliner marked a significant moment for hip-hop and Black culture. Historically, Super Bowl halftime shows have leaned toward pop and rock genres, with limited representation of hip-hop artists. By selecting Lamar, the NFL acknowledged the genre's cultural dominance and its importance as a voice for social issues.

Lamar's performance was a testament to the resilience, creativity, and influence of Black artists in the music industry. His collaboration with other artists, such as SZA and Mustard, further highlighted the contributions of Black creatives to contemporary music and culture. Serena Williams' appearance during the performance added another layer of representation, as she is one of the most celebrated Black female athletes in history.

Addressing Social Issues Through Art

Kendrick Lamar is known for his thought-provoking lyrics and powerful social commentary. His song choices for the halftime show subtly addressed issues such as identity, inequality, and resilience. The inclusion of Samuel L. Jackson's portrayal of Uncle Sam during the show was a bold artistic decision that symbolized patriotism while also questioning America's history of social injustices.

The performance did not explicitly delve into politics, but the underlying themes resonated with viewers who recognized the significance of the imagery and messages. This approach demonstrated the power of art to spark conversations and inspire change without alienating a diverse audience.

The Role of Sports in Bridging Cultural Divides

The Super Bowl has long been a unifying event that brings together people from different backgrounds, political views, and cultural experiences. Super Bowl LIX was no exception. Despite ongoing societal divisions, the event provided a moment of collective joy and excitement. The game itself, featuring two competitive teams, and the entertainment elements demonstrated the power of sports to bridge cultural divides and create a shared experience.

Fans from across the United States and beyond gathered in living rooms, sports bars, and stadium seats to watch the event. Social media was abuzz with reactions to key plays, halftime performances, and special guest appearances. This global engagement underscored the Super Bowl's ability to foster a sense of community and solidarity.

Influence on Pop Culture

The halftime show, game highlights, and memorable moments from Super Bowl LIX quickly became cultural touchstones. Serena Williams' dance performance went viral, sparking countless memes and social media posts. Kendrick Lamar's choice of songs and the appearance of Samuel L. Jackson became topics of discussion on news platforms and social media alike.

The influence extended beyond just the entertainment world. Lamar's performance reignited conversations about the role of music in addressing societal issues. His bold and unapologetic approach to art inspired other artists to use their platforms for meaningful expression.

A Platform for Change

The social and cultural impact of Super Bowl LIX went beyond entertainment. It served as a reminder that sports and music have the power to influence societal norms and challenge the status quo. The event highlighted the importance of representation, the need for ongoing conversations about social issues, and the value of diverse voices in shaping culture.

By embracing hip-hop, celebrating diversity, and acknowledging the contributions of various cultural icons, Super Bowl LIX set a precedent for future events. It demonstrated that sports and entertainment can be powerful tools for social change, inspiring audiences to reflect, engage, and contribute to a more inclusive and equitable society.

A Lasting Legacy

Super Bowl LIX will be remembered not only for the game itself but also for its cultural and social significance. The event left a lasting legacy that transcended the field, reminding us that sports and entertainment are more than just pastimes — they are reflections of our society, capable of inspiring progress and unity. As viewers look back on this historic event, its social and cultural impact will continue to resonate for years to come.

Chapter 6: Post-Game Celebrations and Legacy

Player and Coach Reactions

The final whistle of Super Bowl LIX not only signaled the conclusion of an exhilarating game but also marked the beginning of intense emotional responses from players, coaches, and fans. The triumph of the Philadelphia Eagles and the fierce competition displayed by the Kansas City Chiefs culminated in heartfelt celebrations, emotional interviews, and reflections that painted a vivid picture of the significance of this historic moment. Both teams' reactions underscored the hard work, determination, and resilience that defined their journey to the Super Bowl.

Eagles' Ecstatic Celebration

The Philadelphia Eagles' victory was met with unrestrained joy and celebration. Players embraced on the field, many shedding tears of happiness as they realized the magnitude of their accomplishment. Quarterback Jalen Hurts, who had played a pivotal role throughout the season and the game, was visibly emotional during his post-game interview. Having overcome challenges and doubts early in his career, Hurts spoke passionately about the team's perseverance and his gratitude for the support from coaches and teammates.

"It's not just about winning a game — it's about proving that hard work, unity, and belief can take you anywhere," Hurts said. "This team never gave up, and I'm just proud to be part of this journey."

Head coach Nick Sirianni was equally jubilant. As a relatively new coach in the league, Sirianni's leadership had been questioned initially, but he proved his critics wrong by guiding the Eagles to a Super Bowl victory. In his post-game remarks, Sirianni expressed immense pride in his players and coaching staff. "These guys played their hearts out. We faced adversity all season long, but we stuck together, and tonight we showed the world what Eagles football is all about."

Kansas City Chiefs: Grace in Defeat
On the other side, the Kansas City Chiefs handled their defeat with grace and composure. Quarterback Patrick Mahomes, known for his competitive spirit and sportsmanship, acknowledged the Eagles' impressive performance while expressing disappointment in the outcome.

"Of course, we wanted to win, but hats off to the Eagles. They played a great game and deserved this victory," Mahomes said. "This is just fuel for us. We'll come back stronger next season."

Head coach Andy Reid, a veteran coach with a wealth of experience, also addressed the media with poise. Despite the loss, Reid emphasized the team's resilience and determination throughout the season. "I'm proud of these guys. They fought hard, and even though it didn't go our way tonight, I know we have the talent and heart to come back stronger."

Reid's message of optimism resonated with Chiefs fans, who were already looking forward to the next season with hopes of reclaiming their championship status.

Notable Player Reactions

Several players from both teams shared their thoughts and emotions after the game. Eagles wide receiver DeVonta Smith, who made crucial plays throughout the game, emphasized the team's bond as a key factor in their success. "We have each other's backs, no matter what. That's what got us here, and that's what won us this championship," he said.

Chiefs tight end Travis Kelce, a fan favorite known for his energetic personality, was candid in his assessment of the game. "It hurts, no doubt. But we learn from this, and we keep pushing. That's what champions do," Kelce remarked.

Eagles defensive lineman Fletcher Cox, one of the team's veteran players, highlighted the historical significance of the win. "This is for the city of Philadelphia. We've been through ups and downs, but this moment is for all the fans who've stood by us," he declared.

A Victory for the Fans
The reactions from players and coaches extended beyond the field and resonated deeply with fans. The city of Philadelphia erupted in celebration, with thousands of fans taking to the streets to revel in the team's victory. Chants of "Fly Eagles Fly" echoed throughout the city as fans celebrated their team's triumph.

On social media, the hashtag #EaglesChampions trended for hours, with fans sharing their joy, congratulatory messages, and memorable moments from the game. The outpouring of support demonstrated the deep connection between the team and its passionate fan base.

Chiefs fans, though disappointed, expressed pride in their team's journey and voiced their support for future success. The sportsmanship displayed by both fan bases highlighted the unifying power of football.

Coaches' Reflections on Legacy

As the dust settled, both Nick Sirianni and Andy Reid reflected on the legacy of their respective teams. Sirianni spoke about the importance of building a lasting culture of success. "This is just the beginning for us. We want to build something special here in Philadelphia, something that lasts for years to come," he said.

Reid, known for his wisdom and experience, shared his belief in the Chiefs' ability to maintain their competitive edge. "We've built a winning culture here, and one game doesn't change that. We'll learn from this and come back stronger," he affirmed.

A Historic Super Bowl

Super Bowl LIX will be remembered not only for its thrilling gameplay but also for the emotional reactions and inspiring reflections from players and coaches. The victory for the Eagles cemented their place in football history, while the Chiefs' gracious response highlighted the resilience and character that define champions.

As fans look back on this momentous event, the reactions from those who lived it will remain a testament to the power of sports to inspire, unite, and create lasting memories. The legacy of Super Bowl LIX is not just in the final score but in the stories of perseverance, triumph, and sportsmanship that will be told for generations to come.

Media and Fan Responses

The aftermath of Super Bowl LIX was marked by a flurry of media coverage and passionate reactions from fans across the globe. From post-game analysis and social media trends to heartfelt fan celebrations, the event captured the attention and imagination of millions. The reactions from the media and fans highlighted the cultural significance of the game, the dramatic moments on the field, and the impact of the halftime show.

Media Coverage: Headlines and Analysis
In the immediate aftermath of the game, sports networks and media outlets across the United States and beyond published detailed analyses and headlines celebrating the Philadelphia Eagles' victory and dissecting the Kansas City Chiefs' performance. Major networks like ESPN, Fox Sports, and NBC Sports dedicated hours to

post-game breakdowns, player interviews, and expert commentary.

Headlines such as "Eagles Soar to Victory: A Historic Super Bowl Win" and "Jalen Hurts' MVP Performance Seals the Deal" dominated news sites. The media lauded the Eagles' strategic gameplay, resilience, and standout performances from key players, particularly Jalen Hurts, who was named the game's MVP.

In addition to praising the Eagles, analysts highlighted the Chiefs' efforts, with many commending Patrick Mahomes' leadership and determination despite the loss. Analysts emphasized that Mahomes remained one of the league's elite quarterbacks and predicted that the Chiefs would remain strong contenders in future seasons.

The halftime show, headlined by Kendrick Lamar, also garnered significant media attention. Critics praised Lamar's powerful and socially conscious performance, which struck a balance between entertainment and cultural commentary. Entertainment news outlets described it as "one of the most impactful Super Bowl halftime shows in recent history."

Fan Reactions: A Tale of Two Cities

The reactions from fans were as diverse as the game itself. In Philadelphia, fans flooded the streets to celebrate their team's victory. The city became a sea of green, with fans chanting "Fly Eagles Fly" and waving team flags. Social media was filled with jubilant posts, videos of celebrations, and congratulatory messages for the team.

One fan's viral post summed up the city's emotions: "We waited for this moment, and the Eagles delivered! This win is for every fan who never stopped believing. Let's go, Birds!"

Local bars and restaurants reported record-breaking crowds as fans gathered to watch the game and celebrate the victory. The iconic Rocky Steps at the Philadelphia Museum of Art became a gathering point for fans, who celebrated in true Philadelphia fashion.

In Kansas City, the mood was understandably somber, but fans displayed grace and pride in their team. Social media was filled with messages of support for the Chiefs, with many expressing gratitude for the team's efforts and optimism for the future.

One Chiefs fan tweeted: "We didn't get the result we wanted, but we're proud of this team. Mahomes is still our MVP, and we'll be back stronger next year. Chiefs Kingdom forever!"

Social Media Trends and Viral Moments

Super Bowl LIX dominated social media platforms, with hashtags like #SuperBowlLIX, #EaglesChampions, and #FlyEaglesFly trending worldwide. Fans shared their reactions to key plays, controversial calls, and standout performances in real-time. Memes and GIFs flooded Twitter and Instagram, capturing everything from the players' emotional reactions to Kendrick Lamar's halftime show.

One of the most talked-about moments was Serena Williams' surprise appearance during the halftime performance. Fans praised her dance moves and her continued influence as a cultural icon. The viral clip of her energetic performance quickly amassed millions of views and sparked a wave of admiration.

Another viral moment occurred during the game's final moments when Eagles fans captured Jalen Hurts' emotional reaction to the victory. The image of Hurts, with tears in his eyes and a victorious smile, became a symbol of triumph and resilience.

The Power of Community and Sportsmanship
Beyond the excitement and celebration, Super Bowl
LIX showcased the power of sports to bring people
together. Fans from different backgrounds, political
views, and walks of life found common ground in
their love for the game. The shared experience of
watching the Super Bowl created a sense of
community, whether in crowded stadium seats,
living rooms, or online spaces.

Even amid the competitive rivalry between Eagles
and Chiefs fans, there were moments of
sportsmanship and mutual respect. Social media
posts highlighted instances of Eagles fans praising
the Chiefs' efforts and Chiefs fans congratulating
the Eagles on their well-deserved victory.

Impact on Pop Culture and Entertainment
The cultural impact of Super Bowl LIX extended
beyond the game itself. Kendrick Lamar's halftime
performance became a cultural touchstone, inspiring
discussions about representation, artistic expression,
and social commentary in mainstream
entertainment. His setlist, choreography, and
collaborations with other artists were dissected by
music critics and celebrated by fans.

Serena Williams' surprise appearance further
underscored the intersection of sports and

entertainment, solidifying her status as a cultural icon who transcends her achievements on the tennis court.

The event also sparked conversations about the evolving role of the Super Bowl as a platform for cultural expression and social commentary. From Lamar's performance to the representation of diverse voices on and off the field, Super Bowl LIX demonstrated that the event is not just about football but also about reflecting and shaping societal values.

A Lasting Legacy
The media and fan responses to Super Bowl LIX highlighted the event's profound impact on sports, entertainment, and culture. The Eagles' victory, the Chiefs' resilience, and Kendrick Lamar's halftime show left an indelible mark on viewers and participants alike. As fans and analysts continue to reflect on this historic event, its legacy will endure as a testament to the power of sports to inspire, entertain, and unite.

The Legacy of Super Bowl LIX

Super Bowl LIX, held on February 9, 2025, in New Orleans, was a landmark event that left an indelible mark on the NFL and its fans. The Philadelphia

Eagles' decisive 40-22 victory over the Kansas City Chiefs not only secured their championship status but also had far-reaching implications for the league's history, player legacies, and the host community.

Preserving Historical NFL Records

The Chiefs entered Super Bowl LIX with aspirations of becoming the first team since the Green Bay Packers to secure three consecutive Super Bowl victories. However, the Eagles' dominant performance halted this pursuit, ensuring that the Packers remain the only team in NFL history to achieve a three-peat. This outcome preserved a significant historical milestone within the league.

Impact on Player Legacies

For Eagles quarterback Jalen Hurts, this Super Bowl victory solidified his status as one of the premier quarterbacks in the league. His leadership and performance throughout the season culminated in this championship, enhancing his legacy and setting a high standard for future seasons.

Conversely, Chiefs quarterback Patrick Mahomes faced a challenging game, with the Eagles' defense applying relentless pressure that resulted in six sacks and multiple turnovers. This defeat interrupted the Chiefs' dominance and prompted discussions about Mahomes' standing relative to other NFL greats. Comparisons between Mahomes and legendary quarterbacks like Tom Brady were reevaluated in light of this loss.

Community Enrichment Through 'Impact 59'

Beyond the on-field action, Super Bowl LIX left a lasting positive impact on the Greater New Orleans community through the "Impact 59 Powered by Entergy" initiative. This legacy grant program, a collaboration among the New Orleans Super Bowl Host Committee, the New Orleans Saints, the NFL Foundation, and Entergy, was designed to provide enduring support to local nonprofits. The program focused on key areas such as economic development, education, workforce training, youth development, health and wellness, and equity and inclusion. Through Impact 59, over $3.5 million in grants were awarded to 65 organizations, ensuring that the Super Bowl's presence would benefit the community long after the final whistle.

Cultural Significance and Entertainment

The halftime show, headlined by Kendrick Lamar, was lauded for its powerful and socially conscious performance, blending entertainment with cultural commentary. Lamar's setlist and choreography sparked discussions about representation and artistic expression in mainstream entertainment, further cementing the Super Bowl's role as a significant cultural event.

Super Bowl LIX will be remembered not only for the Eagles' triumphant victory and the thwarting of the Chiefs' historic ambitions but also for its lasting contributions to the community and its cultural impact. The game's legacy encompasses preserved NFL records, enhanced player reputations, community enrichment through substantial grants, and a halftime performance that resonated with audiences worldwide. These elements combined to create a multifaceted legacy that will be remembered for years to come.

CONCLUSION

Super Bowl LIX was a landmark event that transcended the boundaries of sports, leaving a legacy that will be remembered for years to come. From the thrilling game itself to the powerful cultural moments and meaningful community initiatives, the event captured the essence of what makes the Super Bowl a globally celebrated spectacle.

The Philadelphia Eagles' historic victory marked a significant chapter in the franchise's history, elevating the careers of players like Jalen Hurts while reasserting the team's dominance in the NFL. The Kansas City Chiefs, despite their defeat, showcased resilience and competitive spirit, further solidifying their place as one of the league's elite teams. The game's tactical depth and pivotal plays will be analyzed by football enthusiasts and experts for seasons to come.

Beyond the game, the halftime show, headlined by Kendrick Lamar, stood as a cultural milestone, blending entertainment with social consciousness. The performance exemplified the growing influence of the Super Bowl as a platform for artistic expression and societal reflection. The presence of iconic guests added another layer of excitement, ensuring that the entertainment segment resonated deeply with viewers.

Furthermore, the "Impact 59" initiative exemplified the enduring community legacy of the event. By awarding millions of dollars in grants to local organizations, the Super Bowl left a positive imprint on the Greater New Orleans area, promoting education, workforce development, health, and equity. This initiative underscored the NFL's commitment to giving back and using its platform to foster positive social change.

The media and fan responses underscored the significance of the event. The passionate reactions, extensive analyses, and widespread social media engagement highlighted how Super Bowl LIX brought together communities, ignited conversations, and created shared memories.

As fans and analysts continue to reflect on the triumphs and challenges of Super Bowl LIX, its legacy will endure as a testament to the power of sports to inspire, entertain, and unite. The event was not just a celebration of athletic excellence but a cultural and social milestone that exemplified the transformative power of the NFL's most iconic event.

Printed in Dunstable, United Kingdom